Unlocking Quantum Relationships

Discovering the Spiritual and Quantum Keys to Wholeness and Connection

by

Dr. Robert Rodich

Unlocking Quantum Relationships

Discovering the Spiritual and Quantum Keys
to Wholeness and Connection

by

Dr. Robert Rodich DD., Ph.D.

9436 Impala Drive

Foley, Alabama 36535

USA

www.DocRodich.com

Unlocking Quantum Relationships

Discovering the Spiritual and Quantum Keys to Wholeness and Connection

ISBN 13 TP: 978-1-962808-16-3

ISBN 13 eBook: 978-1-962808-17-0

Cover Design by Darian Horner Design
(www.darianhorner.com)

Images: 123rf.com #181866926

First Edition: February 2025

10 9 8 7 6 5 4 3 2 1 0

Printed in the United States of America

Table of Contents

Acknowledgments

I would like to thank Lifespring International Ministries and Dr. Ron Horner and Adina Horner for being trailblazers in the Kingdom family. Not only have they provided a platform for many of us, but they have also been there to encourage me every step of the way. Their staff has been incredible in assisting in making sure the material presented in my books is legible and presentable.

It has been a great blessing to have a resource to send people to for advocacy sessions, knowing that I can only do so much. I highly recommend that the reader visit their website at RonHorner.com to find a wealth of information that will assist the reader in his or her walk.

Every time a series of heavenly downloads is turned into a book, there are many to thank. Among these are the heavenly messengers we rarely see yet are so faithful to make sure they do the warfare needed to see we get the information. Also, all the people who continue to be a source of encouragement and inspiration to me—clearly, this is a key time in human history, and we need each other on so many levels.

Recommendations

This remarkable entry from Dr. Robert Rodich is a must-read for everyone who hungers for the profound significance of nurturing intimacy with the Lord. It beautifully reveals how prioritizing our relationship with God first is beneficial and essential in overcoming the obstacles that hinder us in our daily lives. Within this captivating piece, part of a series exploring quantum revelations, readers are bound to uncover invaluable wisdom that resonates on many levels.

Dr. Rodich has a unique and eloquent teaching style that allows him to communicate the deeper truths of the Kingdom of Heaven in an accessible and engaging way. His insights paint a vivid picture of the journey toward building a strong identity through transformative encounters with Heaven. The revelations shared in this book not only inspire but also offer practical guidance that can empower readers to break free from the long-standing oppression that may have held them captive for far too long.

Join in this enlightening exploration and let Dr. Rodich's teachings motivate you to seize these life-changing revelations. Embrace the chance to rejuvenate your spirit as you uncover the abundant life that awaits you through a closer relationship with God. This heartfelt invitation to grow closer to the Lord offers a path filled with hope and transformation. Don't miss out on the opportunity to engage with these life-shifting insights!

Jeremy Friedman
Director,
Heaven Down™ Business, Inc.
HeavenDownBusiness.com

Foreword

A Profound and Transformative Exploration
of Quantum Relationships

It is with great admiration that I recommend *Unlocking Quantum Relationships,* a deeply insightful and revelatory work that speaks with great integrity about our divine connection and purpose. In this book, Dr. Robert Rodich masterfully unpacks the concept of quantum relationships—specifically, our relationship with our Heavenly Father—and how we were never meant to remain entangled with the Tree of the Knowledge of Good and Evil. Instead, we were designed for something far greater: to walk in restored governmental authority on the earth.

With wisdom and clarity, Dr. Rodich illuminates the truth that we are carriers of divine light—light that is not only spiritual but profoundly quantum in nature. As sons and daughters of God, we have the capacity to shift reality, to bring transformation, and to partner with Heaven in changing the trajectory of humanity. The earth itself groans in anticipation of our awakening, yearning for us to step into our rightful place as bearers of divine influence.

This book is not just a theological discourse—it is a call to action. It challenges us to rise beyond mere knowledge and into true kingdom authority, restoring the balance of Heaven on earth. If you are seeking a deeper understanding of your divine identity and the limitless power within you, *Unlocking Quantum Relationships* is an essential read.

Prepare to be challenged, empowered, and awakened to the reality that you are light, you are quantum, and you are called to shift the world in your quantum relationships.

> *Stephanie Stanfill*
> Chief Operating Officer,
> LifeSpring International
> Ministries, Inc.

Introduction

Recently, I have been pondering why so many believers have had issues with clear biblical truth, behaviors, and protocols. While there is not one simple answer to my query, what the Lord did impress upon my understanding is that it is all about relationships—relationship first with their Creator, then with their self, and then with others.

People who fail to grasp key bits of understanding and who fail to fully embrace the process of denying self are going to struggle. Failure to do so leaves one vulnerable to social and cultural expectations that are not necessarily biblical.

There is no substitute for a deep personal relationship with the Creator. Relationship with Him sets the stage for how well we are able to remove the filters and static of life and, once removed, how well we are able to engage Heaven to receive all the resources necessary to walk out our earthly assignment.

Once we are born of water and the Spirit (born from above), we are an entirely new creation. The goal is then to actualize all that is available to us as new creations. Frankly, this is easier said than done. Working our salvation out with fear and trembling is the process by which we replace the default tendencies of the flesh with God's light and presence in every part of our nature. The measure of success we achieve in this process determines how successful we will be as we address the assignments we all have. We are all called to be ambassadors of Heaven so that God's will is done on Earth as it is in Heaven.

The focus of this work is to point out the process and resources that are available to us so we can fulfill our assignments and that this same process also works to help us build and enhance all the relationships we have in life.

We must lock into the fact that every true human is on Earth on assignment. We played a role in choosing the time we came to Earth, what we look like and what challenges we may face in our Earth journey.

We are born into an earthly family that comes with generational baggage and the universal curse placed upon humanity caused by the fall in Eden. Fortunately, when the timing was right, God sent His one and only Son to establish a single pathway to restoration. That pathway comes with heavenly access to God's presence and all of heaven's resources.

It is vital to get a grasp of that single pathway because two systems are competing for our attention. The system embodied by the Tree of the Knowledge of Good and Evil *(Bad Tree)* seeks to put us on an alternate timeline. It is a system of seduction and abuse. And a system that uses those under its influence and then eliminates them when their usefulness is no longer needed.

The approved system is the one embodied by the Tree of Life. This system is one of life, wholeness, peace, purpose, and relationship with the person of our actual Creator. Unlike the competing system that focuses on a nebulous universal "god consciousness" and the 'you are a "mini-god"' directive, the Tree of Life restores a person to their true family with nothing but the best of intentions. This is the highest possible relationship.

In this book, we will be looking at relationships from a quantum perspective. While I laid out the case for quantum in my book *Unlocking the Quantum Kingdom*,[1] we will first

---

[1] Scroll Publishers (2024).

revisit the basics of quantum and then see how these principles can assist us to build a stronger relationship with God, our self, and then others.

I am convinced that many people lack the understanding of just how special they are in God's view. I also believe that a deeper understanding of why we are here is necessary to build confidence in our assignment. A greater understanding helps us walk in solidarity with God's overall plan. Perhaps we need to be reminded we are who we are because of who our Savior is.

While traditional Christianity focuses on "rules and performance," Kingdom focuses on our standing exemplified by God's grace and love. Often, by default, the former promotes soul dominance while the latter urges the believer to live by the Spirit with the greatest possible liberty in a relationship. Being anchored in the Father's love grants access to His heart and grounds us as little else can.

The process of allowing the Holy Spirit to clear out spiritual legalities, filters, static, and trauma from our life should be considered boot camp training that serves as a foundation for the things we will be able to impart to others. Let's see how this lines up with new creation realities and the quantum grid that God put in place as a resource to address the cry of creation. Then, we will be able to bless the lives of those in our sphere of influence.

Chapter 1
Quantum Basics

Quantum physics is a branch of science that explores the hidden principles governing observable reality. It reveals that behind what we see, unseen forces operate beyond space and time, often unnoticed under normal conditions. These quantum phenomena are sometimes described as "spooky" because they defy the straightforward cause-and-effect explanations typically taught in school.

To say the least, the discovery of quantum principles has rocked traditional science to its core. The problem traditional science is having is that what quantum reveals is almost spiritual, which flies in the face of their evolutionary beliefs.

In my book *Unlocking the Quantum Kingdom,* I point out that the Bible is full of quantum examples. Translocation, quantum entanglement, and bilocation (Christ in us) are just a few examples. It is even possible that some miracles, which involve manifesting higher dimensional realities on Earth, are quantum principles in action.

For example:

39 When they came up out of the water, the Spirit of the Lord [suddenly] took Philip [and carried him] away [to a different place]; and the eunuch no longer saw him, but he went on his way rejoicing. 40 But Philip found himself at Azotus, and as he passed through he preached the good news [of salvation] to all the cities, until he came to Caesarea [Maritima]. (Acts 8:39-40)

10 Do you not believe that I am in the Father, and the Father is in Me? The words I say to you I do not say on My own initiative or authority, but the Father, abiding continually in Me, does His works [His attesting miracles and acts of power]. 11 Believe Me that I am in the Father and the Father is in Me; otherwise believe [Me] because of the [very] works themselves [which you have witnessed]. 12 I assure you and most solemnly say to you, anyone who believes in Me [as Savior] will also do the things that I do; and he will do even greater things than these [in extent and outreach], because I am going to the Father. (John 14:10-12)

God [in His eternal plan] chose to make known to them how great for the Gentiles are the riches of the glory of this mystery, which is Christ in and among you, the hope and guarantee of [realizing the] glory. (Colossians 1:27)

It is like quantum requires us to build a new reality to operate in it. A new reality can be a difficult concept for those who have spent a lifetime reacting to what they naturally observe. The purpose of this book is to consider how quantum mechanics and principles could be used to address interpersonal relationships better.

For example, let's say we have a confrontation at work. We may think that person is just having a bad day or that they may be self-centered. While this may be true, there can often be a much deeper back story, a back story connected to multiple unseen forces that we are not used to thinking about.

Quantum awareness enables us to understand that the streams of life may have more going on than what we observe with our eyes. As believers, we are designed to see, know, feel, and hear at a much deeper level than we often do. Quantum may be an avenue worth pursuing that will equip us to better demonstrate God's Kingdom here on Earth. To quote the beloved Paul Harvey, quantum may help us see "the rest of the story."

Science recognizes that we are energetic beings, and we know that we are made in God's image. In my book *Unlocking the Quantum Kingdom,* I point out that there is more going on around us than the traditional electromagnetic system that we were forced to think was the gold standard of modern science.

Shockingly, God's Word lines up exactly with a quantum principle called magnetoelectric. In simple terms, magnetoelectricity describes the relationship between electric and magnetic fields and scientists have been able to show they are deeply connected. This principle reflects how God spoke creation into existence and offers a scientific glimpse into how unseen forces sustain the physical world.

Those of us with a Kingdom mindset understand that as His *boots on the ground,* we are to use magneto-electric to carry out any assignment He gives us. This means we are imparting the higher dimensional principles of creation into the design of 3-D reality as we say them out loud.

Quantum physics tells us that light and sound are the same thing. Because scripture tells us that we are the light of the world, as we speak and release well-sourced and confident words (speech), we are to change things around us. We are called to displace darkness with light in people, places, commerce, education and government. We are called to impart the very designs of Heaven into Earth.

> *[14] You are the light of [Christ to] the world. A city set on a hill cannot be hidden; [15] nor does anyone light a lamp and put it under a basket, but on a lampstand, and it gives light to all who are in the house. [16] Let your light shine before men in such a way that they may see your good deeds and moral excellence, and [recognize and honor and] glorify your Father who is in heaven. (Matthew 5:14-16)*

With quantum being both a delivery system and a source of creative material, we are no longer dependent on our skills of persuasion as the only way to affect a change in people. It's really important to know that God put a system in place to help us with our assignment, which is to cause everything we come into contact with to operate at a higher level. What we are really discussing here is our ability to govern. To govern properly a person has to know the boundaries of that governance and also the possibilities that may result from governing properly.

We are also freed from hoping that God will somehow sovereignly change every situation. For reasons only known to Him, He decided to include us in the greater process of restoration. While He is free to change any situation at His pleasure, He may assign you or me to address a situation as well. To do so means we need to know what is at our disposal and firmly believe we are called to be *change agents* here on Earth. Those who accept the fullness of this challenge will see that in order to operate at the highest possible level, there must be an uncommon dedication to walk in honor, integrity, holiness, truth, and His love. And this is not possible until we fully know who we are and see ourselves as He sees us.

May I remind you that the majority of Christianity is focused on getting people saved and eventually to Heaven. Kingdom folks affirm this and much more. We take very literally, "Thy Kingdom come and will be done on earth as it is in heaven." We are also aware that multiple sources of opposition exist, including those who believe the Kingdom is only for the millennial reign. With this in mind, we press forward into a Kingdom dynamic that points out that we must expand our thinking in order to see "greater things than these."

> *Your kingdom come, Your will be done on earth as it is in Heaven. (Matthew 6:10)*

Chapter 2
A Completely New Order of Being
(A New Identity)

Believers are born from above, being born of water and the Spirit. This speaks of us as a **totally new** being that is formatted after the second Adam who is our Lord and Savior Jesus Christ. This means we are a part of a higher realm and also a part of a higher resource base.

> *Therefore if anyone is in Christ [that is, grafted in, joined to Him by faith in Him as Savior], he is a new creature [reborn and renewed by the Holy Spirit]; the old things [the previous moral and spiritual condition] have passed away. Behold, new things have come [because spiritual awakening brings a new life]. (2 Corinthians 5:17)*

Clearly, this is a platform of operation that is very different from what we are used to in Earth-based 3-D reality.

So different, in fact, that it is like trying to hook up a 110-voltage system with power intended for a 220-voltage system. It takes a completely different type of wire to accommodate that increased level of power.

This new system is based outside of space and time as we know it. The good news is that we have the directions to put this whole thing together. Those directions are sourced from the book we call the Holy Bible. God's Word points out how to replace any potential blockages that the system we were born into may place upon us. It also points out how to connect to the new, as it helps build a much higher set of expectations.

This new system we are a part of is one of very powerful light. The old system we were born into masquerades as a system of light when, in reality, it is one of deception, chaos and bondage. The old system also promotes self and a connection to a nebulous universe as our source. The heavenly system focuses on restoration to our Creator, His plan for our life, our earthly assignment, and the resources necessary to complete our assignment. Really, we become a part of a higher order.

Water is an excellent conductor of electricity. In the same way, those who are born from above are dynamically connected to the flow of **Living Water**—the life-giving presence of God. This divine connection allows our inner being to carry a spiritual current that natural water cannot.

Being born of the Spirit grants us access to the Holy Spirit and attunes our spirit to a higher design. Through this transformation, the Holy Spirit becomes our resident teacher and the ultimate source of truth, guiding us into deeper understanding and purpose.

He who believes in Me [who adheres to, trusts in, and relies on Me], as the Scripture has said, 'From his innermost being will flow continually rivers of living water.' (John 7:38)

While the opposing system promises enlightenment, it simply cannot deliver the same way that the approved system can. The real question here is are we satisfied with the way we are, or do we believe what God says about us?

What we're discussing is transitioning from a "milk" mentality to a "meat" mentality, as the Apostle Paul describes. This means maturing and growing into the Kingdom with purpose. It's a crucial shift in understanding as we build a new reality—one powerful enough for us to speak into and transform both our environment and vital relationships.

Chapter 3
Frequency Doesn't Lie

Being fully committed to Jesus in relationship also speaks of accountability that then leads to doing greater things than these. I am reminded that we cannot give what we do not contain. To complete the change within ourselves, to affect others, and to govern requires a resident foundation that supports what we put on that foundation. To operate fully in quantum, that foundation needs to be stronger than most people think.

Throughout my lifetime, I have met thousands of people, most of whom were sincere in who they were. Some, however, were all talk and very little substance. Words alone have little effect when it comes to engaging quantum and even less of an effect while engaging the essence of creation without sanctified intention and purposeful emotion.

The reason I highlight personal intimacy *with the Lord in all my writings is that I know that the time we spend with Him is where we gain the light, perspective, and authority needed to engage the quantum system with honor and integrity. How else do we put ourself into a position to only do what we see the Father do?* (John 5:19)

For the past 1900 years, we have had access to the teachings of the Bible, yet if we look at the effect that believers have had on humanity as a whole, it has been anemic at best. So, we have to ask how that has worked out for us. Or we should ask if a deeper commitment is required on our part to *first* walk in a greater revelation of God's Word and, *second*, demonstrate the fullness of that word so that we do shake things up as we are supposed to be doing. For some, this will require adopting a new reality.

Adopting a new reality is defined as seeking God to the point where we ask Him to reveal His plan and its depth, so we see it His way. Part of that revelation is to only do what we see the Father do. This is in contrast to going outside of approved revelation, as some are doing. Perhaps they, too, are not seeing results the traditional way; however, contacting spirit guides or connecting to the universe is not where we should be going.

Let's be mindful that the great end-time deception is likely to be other dimensional beings passing themselves off as the "so-called aliens" who created us. They may show up with technology and mystical energies that could fool even God's elect if that were possible. This is especially noteworthy for those who hold experiences as the standard for advanced spirituality, so I caution all of us to be careful. Other dimensional beings would love to entice us with "mystical" experiences to throw us off of the true pathway.

> [25] 'There will be signs (attesting miracles) in the sun and moon and stars; and on the earth [there will be] distress and anguish among nations, in perplexity at the roaring and tossing of the sea and the waves, [26] people fainting from fear and expectation of the [dreadful] things coming on the world; for the [very] powers of the heavens will be shaken. [27] Then they will see THE SON OF MAN COMING IN A CLOUD with [transcendent, overwhelming] power [subduing the nations] and with great glory. [28] Now when these things begin to occur, stand tall and lift up your heads [in joy], because [suffering ends as] your redemption is drawing near.' [29] Then He told them a parable: 'Look at the fig tree and all the trees; [30] as soon as they put out leaves, you see it and know for yourselves that summer is near. [31] So you too, when you see these things happening,

know [without any doubt] that the kingdom of God is near.' (Luke 21:25-31)

I suggest taking the time to be so familiar with Father's heart that when you leave that engagement, you can't help but set the world around you on fire. Some of us just need to go there and not leave until we are totally rewired and changed on every level. His heart is where we were birthed; it is our place of rest, and it is our home. How easily we forget!

Living in His presence is how we set the standard for what we are able to contain and then give to others. Let us be patient and do it His way and not jump ahead and then fall to the ground in a heap of ashes. Failure to spend the time to develop such intimacy allows many filters and static to stay in place that skew the things God could speak to us. As creation is groaning, it is calling out for clarity not mixture or the best of carnal intentions. And creation simply will not respond to those who are full of themselves, carnally or religiously.

Light emits frequency, and frequency does not lie. We need to understand this if our goal is to do greater things than those that Jesus said were possible. Frequency is what opens the unseen portals into quantum and gives us access to 100% of what the quantum grid is capable of. Another way to put it is that creation and Heaven only respond to the level of authenticity we contain. In all dimensions, that authenticity is measured by the energy (vibes, frequency) we release from our person.

Let's be reminded that Wi-Fi, AM, and FM signals are all around us and actually go through us all the time. These signals are unseen; however, it doesn't mean they are not there. Just because they are unseen doesn't mean that the thoughts and intentions we release aren't being broadcasted out from us. And as we release them, they have the potential to affect much more than we think.

It takes a radio tuner to convert radio signals into something we can listen to. Quantum is full of signals from Heaven and creative potential. Perhaps what God is trying to do to us is turn us into *tuner-like* beings that can convert the potential contained in quantum into something visible on Earth. The enemy's camp has had its shot for approximately 6,000 years, so now it's our turn.

To further demonstrate what I am talking about, have you ever been in a situation where a certain person enters a room, and the room just lights up? That person is putting out frequency waves (energy) that affect the atmosphere in a way so as to create a positive or engaging environment. And clearly, the energy is palpable. Most of us normally respond positively.

How about a person who enters the room, and they seem to suck all the energy out of that room? Or a troubled person entering the room, and you can just tell something isn't right? We normally comment that this person gives off bad vibes.

Everyone has a story, and we often broadcast that story without even thinking about it. We need to understand that our story can have multiple energetic layers attached to it. The more emotionally charged our energy is then, the more powerful the effect will be. And it doesn't stop there! Energy has the potential to bless in so many ways if we carry it responsibly.

My question to you is, "What are you broadcasting knowingly or unknowingly"? This is an important question to address because if what you are broadcasting is emotionally charged in any way, you will attract more of the same from the mechanical spectrum of the quantum grid.

For as he thinks in his heart, so is he [in behavior—one who manipulates]. He says to you, 'Eat and drink,' Yet his heart is not with you [but it is begrudging the cost]. (Proverbs 23:7)

The mechanical side of the quantum grid has memory and can hold the energetic signature of things, good or bad. Since its purpose seems to be to assist us in our co-creative assignments then we need to make cleaning up traumas, poor emotions, and bad behaviors a top priority. These are what I term as filters and static to include spiritual legalities as well. Scientifically speaking, with less resistance in place, the greater the potential exists to conduct in its highest possible expression exactly what God sends our way.

Spiritual legalities include familial and personal agreements like vows, soul ties, and, in extreme cases, human sacrifices done in the past to put a person in a position of evil power. Both the grid and our person can house the energetic value of these. The same could be said for the mechanical side of the grid and our person containing love, joy, peace, kindness, and other positive traits. The goal is to switch off the negative and enable a positive flow that comes directly from the heart of the Father.

You shall not worship them nor serve them; for I, the LORD your God, am a jealous (impassioned) God [demanding what is rightfully and uniquely mine], visiting (avenging) the iniquity (sin, guilt) of the fathers on the children [that is, calling the children to account

for the sins of their fathers], to the third and fourth
generations of those who hate Me. (Exodus 20:5)

Based on quantum principles, it is clear that few people give thought to the possibility that they may be broadcasting good or bad things that affect other people and, therefore, their potential relationships with them. Also of interest is the fact that these same issues serve as energetic filters that may skew the way a person processes information. Should that be the case, there seems to be a pride factor built in that keeps a person from reasonably being honest about self. Let's be reminded that these same energies can also attract things, good or bad, from the quantum grid.

As an example, a person may feel they never get a break or that they are being singled out for no good reason. Likely, that person is unaware that they may be attracting the very things that make them feel uncomfortable. Another example is why certain folks seem to attract only the bad people or people who turn out to be projects in their relationships.

While the list of scenarios could be much longer, it is clear that once a person has been born from above, they have the power to make better choices, change how they think, and alter what they attract. Actions have consequences, and so do our choices. Now, we are beginning to see that there is

18

a grid and unseen principles in place that explain why so many reap the whirlwind while others reap exceptional blessings.

Chapter 4
Life Experiences Can Create Filters

The goal of this book is to encourage the reader to think outside of the box when it comes to relationships and to point out that when we have expanded our thinking, there are resources available that are quite different than those we naturally default to.

Our soul is the processing center for the majority of interpersonal frequency exchanges. It also serves as our gatekeeper, protecting us from excessive harm by evaluating each frequency that carries intent and emotion. Additionally, the soul is the place where the effects of trauma are stored.

If left unaddressed, trauma runs like a faulty program in the background. *(This may explain why years of counseling and various programs often yield only limited success. Unless those bad programs—and their frequency signatures—are eliminated, a person may remain trapped in cycles of repeated frustration.)*

When a person says that another person has hurt them, and they are determined never to let it happen again they are establishing a shield. That shield can also serve as a filter. We observe this when someone offers remarks on certain topics where their demeanor seems jaded. The list of potential examples here is almost endless. However, I think you get the point.

While interaction with others can be challenging at times, so too is the purposeful programming that comes to our lives through TV, apps, video games, and movies. Without sounding too conspiratorial, we are naive if we think that most things in life are just coincidental. The goal of our enemy is to gaslight us into oblivion so that you and I never come to an understanding of who we are. And certainly, he wants to keep us from experiencing God's goodness.

So, the game plays on. If the enemy cannot attract us to outright evil, then they will try to direct our focus to material things. Status and what we have is in direct opposition to "who" we have. If we have the Lord and are fully committed to His plan for our life, then what we need to fulfill our assignment will flow very naturally. This is a critical point to understand because rather than focusing on personal or financial survival, should we focus on the "vision" then "provision" is guaranteed? We may own things; however, they will never own us. This goes for material things, status, our accomplishments and even our children.

Why would the enemy of our soul ever want us to know how specially each one of us was created? Why would our enemy want us to know that the way our heavenly Father thinks of us is as if we were the only one He ever created? Should we be able to grasp this, then we will relish spending as much time in His presence as we can, and not just in church. There is a way to spend every moment of the day walking in His presence and still function in daily activities.

I'm reminded of the children of Israel when they were in the process of leaving Egypt. They could have seen all the obstacles as an opportunity to grow closer to God and build an even greater faith at the same time. Most of them couldn't see that all those challenges were put in front of them to get Egypt out of them and also equip them to victoriously take the promised land (boot camp).

Again, this is why I have stated in all three of my books that we cut our teeth on cleaning up ourselves first. Cleaning up self means clearing out the filters and static. It may mean learning how to do heavenly court cases to dissolve any generational legal disputes. It could even call for deliverance in some cases. As we consider these things, we will be confronted with one of the greatest of all filters: PRIDE! While pride can take on many forms we must be aware that pride can stop us cold at any time. This is why humility is of such great value because in our weakness He shows Himself strong.

The promised land represents an entirely new life. An entirely new way of thinking. An entirely new source of energy and inspiration. And a new reality. In our case, it is the place from which we can move the unseen into the visible reality of 3-D Earth, which is our assignment.

Chapter 5
Becoming More Aware
(From Heaven's Perspective)

There is a difference between the *logical mind* and the *intuitive mind.* The logical mind operates by sight, action, rules, logic, and reason, just to name a few. The intuitive mind operates with a heightened awareness of frequencies, intentions, and resources based outside of space and time. In the case of believers, we have a much greater awareness of the spiritual and dimensional realms. Building out the intuitive mind allows us to perceive what our spirit is taking in, yet it doesn't make it through the filter of the natural mind.

As we successfully eliminate filters and static, our awareness often expands exponentially. And because of the way quantum works, information that we once strived to know then begins to flow very easily. The intuitive mind has the potential to be connected to a reality that operates well above the 3-D reality we normally operate in.

> *⁵ Have this same attitude in yourselves which was in Christ Jesus [look to Him as your example in selfless humility], ⁶ who, although He existed in the form and unchanging essence of God [as One with Him, possessing the fullness of all the divine attributes—the entire nature of deity], did not regard equality with God a thing to be grasped or asserted [as if He did not already possess it, or was afraid of losing it]; ⁷ but emptied Himself [without renouncing or diminishing His deity, but only temporarily giving up the outward expression of divine equality and His rightful dignity] by assuming the form of a bond-servant, and being made in the likeness of men [He became completely human but was without sin, being fully God and fully man]. ⁸ After He was found in [terms of His] outward appearance as a man [for a divinely-appointed time], He humbled Himself [still further] by becoming obedient [to the Father] to the point of death, even death on a cross. ⁹ For this reason also [because He obeyed and so completely humbled Himself], God has highly exalted Him and bestowed on Him the name which is above every name, ¹⁰ so that at the name of Jesus EVERY KNEE SHALL BOW [in submission], of those who are in heaven and on earth and under the earth, ¹¹ and that every tongue will confess and openly*

acknowledge that Jesus Christ is Lord (sovereign God),
to the glory of God the Father. (Philippians 2:5-11)

When we finally land on Earth, we are born into a system that finds its foundation in the Tree of the Knowledge of Good and Evil (Bad Tree). This is a system anchored purely in evil and is the antithesis of Heaven itself. This system stands for independence from God by entitling us to make our own decisions.

The energy that this system manifests promotes several levels of dark energy and some that masquerade as light. This includes a "knockoff" version of all that Heaven stands for. Rather than promoting freedom, this dark energy pulls a person into a never-ending spiral of bondage, no matter how enlightening it may seem. We should never underestimate the ability of this platform to fool a person. We must be mindful that because the bad tree system can morph into many forms, it was deceptive enough to entice Eve.

The Tree of Life (Good Tree) stands for all that is good, holy and righteous, including full access to God's very presence. The flow of God's presence is something that we can learn to live in and feed off of. It really is not possible to wear out the potential of what this flow has to offer. What we are now learning is that along with the spiritual, there is tangible science to back up how God manifests His fullness on planet Earth.

The challenge we face is how to build out the intuitive mind. My book *Moving Toward Sonship* defines much of the opposition we face and also gives tips on how to remove it. To build out the intuitive mind we need to acknowledge all the detractors that are in our being. Deal with them and then focus on our standing before God. And what I am speaking of is engaging God's presence in a way that we see ourselves as He sees us. Then, we focus on making this our new reality.

Having addressed these things I asked myself this question, "How do I stop my mind from filtering everything through 3-D reality so that I can know the greater Kingdom reality?" The *brain (mind) creates inner imagery based on the frequencies* that define its reality base. Anything outside of that reality base is filtered out even though we are taking in far more information than we realize.

The best example of how our natural mind can filter things is a video I watched about a gorilla running across a basketball court. The people in the stands were told only to watch the team in white. Those who did never saw the gorilla, even though it was plainly visible in the video. Because of what they were told the fact that the gorilla was plainly visible never registered in their minds. I find that amazing.

Naturally speaking, 3-D earth reality is something we grow into and accept as normal. Those who practice "new age" or "new thought" (positive thinking) are trying to break free and rise above 3-D. What they fail to realize is that the process they are embracing is only moving them deeper into the "Bad Tree" system.

There are those in the body of Christ who are being fooled by this as well. They confuse the "enlightenment" they experience as being the same as that which comes from God's presence. Their inability to rightly judge their "mystical" experiences may be why so many of them eventually embrace universalism.

Then, some think any attempt to replace the frequency base that the brain uses to process frequency into imagery is inherently evil, so they dismiss the need completely. These folks usually default to intellectual Christianity leaving them subject to performance and legalism. The result is that they end up missing out on the operational shift necessary to see, know, hear, and feel clearly in the Kingdom.

And set your minds and keep them set on what is above (the higher things), not on the things that are on the earth. (Colossians 3:2)

This scripture is yet another quantum reference. "*SET your minds on things above*"—this is where the frequencies are that can build out a greater and new reality, renewing our mind (intuitive). This truth was there all along, hiding in plain sight. WOW!!! Another reason to hang out with Father. Being in Him is where the ultimate reality is! This is like finding the missing link. Replace the frequency base that defines what the mind accepts as reality, and we are no longer outsiders trying to look in. We just need to make sure we are connecting to the correct frequency base.

God's Word and being in His heart help us acquire a new frequency/reality base for our mind to replace the set of 3-D frequencies we know so well. The answer to how we build an intuitive mind is to set our mind on things above. As we do that, we can focus on accepting a new set of frequencies that will fully connect us to new creation realities.

Chapter 6
The Enemy's Plan

The enemy intends to craft a narrative that is close enough to the truth to draw people in, ensnare them, and make us believe we're on the right track. The plan is designed to strip humanity of the authority God gave to Adam. This is accomplished by exploiting legal gateways, which are either established through generations or by our consent. They then will drain off our authority as well as our personal energy and vitality. The ultimate goal is to eliminate humanity entirely, which is the most powerful way they can hurt God. This is because all humans are the apple of His eye.

¹ Now the serpent was more crafty (subtle, skilled in deceit) than any living creature of the field which the LORD God had made. And the serpent (Satan) said to the woman, 'Can it really be that God has said, "You shall not eat from any tree of the garden"?' ² And the woman said to the serpent, 'We may eat fruit from the trees of the garden, ³ except the fruit from the tree which is in the middle of the garden. God said, "You shall not eat from it nor touch it, otherwise you will die."' ⁴ But the serpent said to the woman, 'You certainly will not die! ⁵ For God knows that on the day you eat from it your eyes will be opened [that is, you will have greater awareness], and you will be like God, knowing [the difference between] good and evil.' ⁶ And when the woman saw that the tree was good for food, and that it was delightful to look at, and a tree to be desired in order to make one wise and insightful, she took some of its fruit and ate it; and she also gave some to her husband with her, and he ate. ⁷ Then the eyes of the two of them were opened [that is, their awareness increased], and they knew that they were naked; and they fastened fig leaves together and made themselves coverings. (Genesis 3:1-7)

The warfare against us is real, and the process of that warfare matters. Humankind are the only beings in God's created order that have the authority to change things on planet Earth. Once we have a directive from the Lord to address an issue, it is our words which mirror the way the Father created all things. Those who are free from carnal filters and static pose a very real threat to the enemy's plan. This is why that evil plan is so pervasive and comprehensive.

Free people pose a real and present danger to the enemy's plans.

We see the effects of the evil plan in every aspect of society. The way the institution of the family has been incrementally broken down speaks to this. The arts, education, food production, and religious life have all come under attack. And the disadvantages we inherited as a result of the fall play right into the narrative. Thankfully, there is a way to overcome these disadvantages, even though that way is very narrow.

Those of us fully committed to God's plan must be mindful that part of the plan includes attempts to inject pseudo-religious experiences, hoping we will take the bait. This is a journey, and as with any journey, few of us have reached a point where we are exempt from being sidetracked. We must remain especially cautious of *mystical* and *New Age* practices that promise experiences without the necessary changes required to engage with supernatural experiences God's way.

Let me be clear: those who follow God with their whole heart will have supernatural experiences. On the surface, both genuine and counterfeit experiences may seem similar. It reminds me of fake Rolex watches—they look just like the real thing, yet they are not. I also want to emphasize that we should never fear experiences, because when they arise from a genuine relationship with God, we know they serve a Kingdom purpose.

Additionally, beware of mystical "feel-good" energy, which is often a counterfeit of God's holy presence. His sheep know His voice and can distinguish between His true presence and anything else. Frankly, I do not view what we do as believers as being mystical at all. While what we are called to do may appear outside the usual 3-D Earth way of operating, anything God brings our way should be considered normal Kingdom life.

And finally, be cautious of the "God is the universe" lie. I find it almost laughable that nonbelievers, who can only operate within a small fraction of quantum mechanics, are trying to pass this off as God. (See my book *Unlocking the Quantum Kingdom*.) I suppose when someone only understands 3-D Earth principles, it's easy to be deceived by things that appear supernatural. I can assure you, however, that much of what we will see in the near future will be basic quantum concepts presented as supernatural, especially when our supposed "space progenitors" make their appearance.

Chapter 7
Our Personal Energy Field

Before the fall in Eden, we were beings of incredible light whose body, soul, and spirit operate as one. The fall threw everything into chaos as it introduced an evil alternative system.

Mankind was likely put right in the middle of an already chaotic situation by design. Adam's role was to use his light to change things, speak to things, and restore things. Just imagine what that energy must have looked like and what it could do.

I recently saw an ad for a device that connects to plants and converts their energy into music. They demonstrated it on all kinds of plants, and each one played a unique, beautiful song. As I listened, I couldn't help but wonder—how much more breathtaking would these songs be if Adam had finished the work he was given in the beginning? But then it hit me... we can still continue that work!

I got a deeper picture of what things should be like while listening to a program highlighting believers who have had near-death experiences (NDE). Each said that in Heaven, everything is alive in ways we could only imagine on Earth. They said everything is very expressive. Somehow, each person knew that even the surroundings were glad they were there. Each used terms like "the heavens shouting for joy, mountains singing, hills clothed with gladness, meadows and valleys shouting for joy, the heavens being glad, the sea shouting praise, trees singing for joy."

On Earth, these voices seem silent—except for the device mentioned earlier that can detect the song of plants. In the past, if someone had told me that part of our assignment was to restore creation's song so it could be heard again, I would have thought they were out of their mind. But today, I'm not so sure that's impossible!

Why is creation groaning for the revelation of the sons of God? (Romans 8:19) Just because we assume the fulfillment of this verse is in the distant future doesn't mean we're correct. What if it's possible now?

For [even the whole] creation [all nature] waits eagerly for the children of God to be revealed. (Romans 8:19)

This is part of the problem we face as believers; we assume that present reality should interpret scripture for us. Libraries are full of books written by those interpreting scripture based on 3-D reality. I wonder how many of these really heard directly from God?

Jesus said that you and I are the light of the world. (Matthew 5:14) He also said that if the light in you is darkness how great is that darkness. (Matthew 6:22-23) I have been thrilled over the last several years to see science catch up with a level of technology that proves all that God's word infers about light, energy, and sound. And more revelation is on the way!

You are the light of [Christ to] the world. A city set on a hill cannot be hidden. (Matthew 5:14)

[22] 'The eye is the lamp of the body; so if your eye is clear [spiritually perceptive], your whole body will be full of light [benefiting from God's precepts]. [23] But if your eye is bad [spiritually blind], your whole body will be full of darkness [devoid of God's precepts]. So if the [very] light inside you [your inner self, your heart, your conscience] is darkness, how great and terrible is that darkness! (Matthew 6:22-23)

A look at the Bible shows us examples like the sun standing still, pillars of cloud and fire, sulfur destroying Sodom and Gomorrah, miraculous healings, walking on water and so on. While many of these are miracles by definition, many may also be higher principles being released to supersede the way 3-D Earth operates. The latter is where we come in. Like Adam, we are here on assignment, and once we are restored to the relationship, we can focus on that assignment. We just need to functionally contain the level of authority necessary to release higher Kingdom principles into 3-D earth reality.

We have resources available to build us up, so we become a living resource of Heaven on Earth. To be fully actualized as that resource, we need to have a strong energy field. So why is our energy field so important? Our energy field displays the level of intensity that light and sound are resident within our being. Faith, honor, integrity and commitment are displayed in our personal space by light and sound. There is only one way to increase those levels: intimacy with Jesus by taking communion and spending time with Him.

The more substantially resident that these attributes are in us means they display a more intense light and a more sophisticated sound. Very sophisticated photography and those who know how to operate beyond the norms of 3-D Earth reality can also observe light and sound operate in people. Do you recall I stated that sound and frequency do not lie? Our own personal force field is what sends the enemy packing or does not. The same field also determines to what depth we may interact with quantum and how clearly we release design to that which is around us.

I recently watched a video produced by Japanese scientists. In that video, they had equipment that captured the energy coming out of a lady. Initially, it was beams of light; however, when her young daughter entered the picture, the waves changed from beams of light to concentric circles. Do you suppose the waves were surrounding waves of love? Finally, scientific understanding is catching up to biblical reality.

In my book *Unlocking the Quantum Kingdom,* I lay out a process by which we are able to move our normal 4 to 5-foot energy field out to 29 feet. At that point, we become more wave than matter, and in that environment, the higher designs of Heaven can be imparted into the Earth. Could it be that you and I are called to rewrite the code of 3-D Earth by imparting higher heavenly designs?

Also of interest is that unlike those who are yet to be redeemed, I believe those born from above are actually released from the chakra-based system of the Tree of the Knowledge of Good and Evil. So then, what does our field look like? We are returned to a torus-like electromagnetic field (more like an oval). This type of field is able to operate on Earth and outside of space and time and is tethered to the Tree of Life.

As support for this, I will share an experience I had several years ago. I was out to dinner with friends, and a lady came up to me, kind of freaked out, and asked me, "Who are you?" I said, "A servant of the Most High." She went on to explain that she could see the auras of everyone in the place except me. I tried to explain that I was no longer a part of the system (matrix) like she was. Also of note is that the video imaging used by the Japanese scientists was only designed to see energy waves and not auras.

So—I ask you, how strong is your energy field?

Chapter 8
Building a New Reality

It has been said that *we don't know what we don't know.* However, once we have been made aware of the greater truth, we must decide if we are going to walk in it or not. This is especially important in these last days as so many believers seem to be half in and half out.

The possibility I am referring to here is being so connected to Heaven, its culture, and its possibilities that we can build a reality of a much higher design than that which we normally operate in. This is especially true of relationships. Wouldn't it be nice to rise above reactive relationships and be able to impart light and life in a way that makes our lives and theirs better? This is why I am providing all this background material to serve as a foundation for the last chapter of this book, which will show us how.

A good place to start is prayer. Prayer shouldn't be focused on what we need but rather on what we do have based on gratitude. Gratitude is a powerful arrow to have in our quill. Gratitude considers something that we know is God's plan for us as already done. This is a really important quantum principle and acts as a faith-building gateway. As we follow Father's directions and then things happen, how can our faith not grow?

3-D Earth reality is very linear and is limited by the speed of light. For example, we must call people if we want to talk to them or travel to see them. This speaks of limits to 3-D Earth operations. In quantum, we just have to think it, and we are there. Remember, in quantum, all possibilities exist at the same time. By God's design, the authority of our voice sparks incredible things. I am sure this is the reality Adam and Eve operated in before the fall. God gave the idea, they spoke it, and boom! It was done.

Adam and Eve's temptation was that something greater than what they had was being hidden from them by God. They found out very quickly this was not the case. Sadly, that "greater reality" was nothing more than the confines of 3-D reality that all the fallen ones were already locked into. Imagine how devastated they must have been once they realized they got scammed!

The good news of the Kingdom is this: because of what Jesus Christ did on the cross, we can be restored to Kingdom possibilities and operations. We have to grow in how we are able to activate these possibilities and in how we operate in the Kingdom. This is as opposed to Adam and Eve being created with all their skills in place. Actually, I think this is a great idea as it keeps us on our toes as we remove the bad programming and replace it with higher programming, literally line upon line. The walk of Kingdom is to build faith and proficiency over time as we remain totally dependent on our Creator.

The foundation of our new reality begins by being deeply rooted in His love. We are called to know it intimately, to rest in it, and to continually draw from it. As we do, we come to recognize that the second Adam—Jesus Christ—reveals a far greater design than the first. He is our living example, firmly established at the core of who we are. In quantum terms, this unity can be described as bilocation: He is in us, and we are in Him (1 John 4:17-18). Through faithful study of our manual—God's Word—our understanding expands, and we realize that we are invited to operate according to this higher design and divine nature.

Chapter 9
The Ultimate Relationship

The time has come for us, as believers, to boldly advance and reclaim what the enemy has stolen. We cannot do this by standing on the sidelines as passive observers; we must be fully engaged. Scripture tells us we are seated with Christ Jesus in heavenly places. When we understand the foundational principles of quantum reality, we begin to see that this is more than a metaphor. Through the concept of bilocation, we are truly present there with Him—both here on earth and seated with Him in the heavenly realm.

> *And He raised us up together with Him [when we believed], and seated us with Him in the heavenly places, [because we are] in Christ Jesus, (Ephesians 2:6)*

Being there means we can build the highest possible relationship with our Creator. It means a new reality and a totally new way to do things—this is now our reality. For years we have heard people testify about what God brought them out of. I think it's time we start hearing testimonies of what God has brought us in to!

We have been restored to the place where we can bask in God's presence continually. This presence should become what we are known for as it fills our energy field out to the max. We cannot hang out with God without it rubbing off on us. As it does, we can't help but begin to see what our assignment is and acquire the faith to do it. All He does, and therefore all we do, must be based on love. Love is a powerful frequency and is capable of affecting profound changes. Frankly, it is love that moves us to repentance, not the fear of punishment. It starts to be fun once we understand this.

As we hang out with Father we get a massive boost in our confidence level. This is also where the intuitive mind is strengthened. It is said that in Heaven, there is no need for speech because everyone can communicate telepathically. Having an in-tune intuitive mind is how we process what God speaks to us. It is hard at first because the natural mind is programmed to process by sight and physical interaction as it filters out things beyond 3-D reality. This is one of many reasons for us to spend time in God's presence so we can overcome the natural mind.

Another aspect of our relationship with the Lord is that He knows all and sees all. He also has the best in mind for us. While I can't answer why bad things happen to good people, I can say that nothing happens outside of God's purview. What I can say is that as we find a home in His heart, we will access advantages that will come no other way.

What we are building toward is the ability to see, know, feel, and hear from a Kingdom point of view. This means that as trusted servants, the Father may well give us a peek into His plan for a spouse, children, as well as friends and acquaintances. Because we are learning quantum possibilities as we build relationship with God, we can now tap into supernatural resource as we build and bless others.

Chapter 10
Relationship with Self

As I have stated, we can't share, release, or impart what we do not possess. The assumption is that we are totally committed to God and His plan for us. We need to understand that naturally, we are not programmed to be game changers to those around us. While we can make life easier by making good choices and being kind and supportive to those around us, let's go beyond just making life easier so we can supernaturally change lives.

Changes in relationship must start with us. Even if we recognize the need for change, the troubling root needs to be found and eliminated. These roots include generational issues passed down to us via DNA and legalities in the spirit realm. Another root can be traumas we have endured that seem to settle in our souls like bad programming running in the background. Family and religious environments can program us very deeply in many ways, including how we think and process information. And I dare not leave out the fact that we are always in a serious spiritual battle purposed to keep us from our assignment. We are born into a war zone.

The world says we need to learn to love ourselves. Unfortunately, this suggestion is often made from a very carnal perspective. Most people do, in fact, focus on themself. The real answer here is to develop that intimacy with Father to the point where we see ourselves the way He sees us. Each one of us was created within the Father Himself. It is quite likely that each of us was designed from an aspect of His DNA, making us a part of Him in a way that few people think about.

We need to lock in on the fact that God made us for a reason. Each one of us is exceptionally unique, so this should help us view ourselves differently. When we see just how loved we really are, we are able to embrace our true selves based on how He sees us. After that, there is no longer a need to perform to earn His love or approval on any level. Then we are free to be about family (His) business.

Because we have established intimacy and because we have seen our real blueprint, we can then move forward to identify any detractors. Becoming a student of the "Living

Word" also keeps the trail fresh as we are tracking down all detractors. Rest assured that the Holy Spirit is ever available to help us in this effort.

Also, there are many resources available that will shed light on how to identify and rid ourselves of things that stand in the way of our goal. The goal is to remove all filters, static, and mindsets that stand in the way of us, establishing an outstanding inner flow of the supernatural (God's light and presence). As we cut our teeth on ridding ourselves of all detractors, we then are positioning ourselves to apply those lessons to those around us.

I recommend that you go to RonHorner.com to find a wealth of resources to address the specifics of what God shows you. Also available are advocate sessions in which the advocates will supernaturally seek a plan on your behalf.

Chapter 11
Putting it All into Action

Let me be clear: we are not learning methodology to control those around us. What we are doing is positioning ourselves to become a game changer to the world around us. Our goal is to take what we have learned and take our improved supernatural sensitivity to invest in those around us.

The first thing I do when I am faced with a relational challenge is go to Father and ask Him to identify the issues and then give me a plan. I also inquire as to the timing of the plan He gives me. Like most things we do in the spirit realm, we build a foundation. We also predetermine not to act out of frustration or impulsively. Choosing to act in love doesn't mean we have to take excessive abuse. What it does mean is that with God's plan in hand, we can step by step implement His plan while tearing down strongholds.

Let me be more specific as I start with spousal relationships. I Let me apologize to the ladies up front for looking at this from a male perspective; however, I am sure you will get something out of the principles I present.

A marriage is two people of different sexes coming together to become one flesh. Another way to look at this is that we need what the other person has. And by this, we are complete. So, let's say there are issues beyond the Mars and Venus thing (a book written years ago about the differences between males and females). We must resist placating just to keep the peace and come up with a life-changing strategy. Remember, we are about restorative change for both parties this time around.

By now, you know how to go directly into God's presence. Go there and ask to see your spouse the way God sees them. Spend some time allowing your heart to be touched by this love He has for your spouse. Then, ask Him for a blueprint. You may need to do a heavenly court case to put restraining orders on generational issues that may be plaguing your spouse. (Dr. Horner's ministry can help with this.) The key is to get strategies from Heaven and then speak them into reality because they came from Father's heart. We also have the authority to do so.

Let's remember that the quantum grid is God's delivery system as a resource transport. Once we have a plan, we need to speak that plan out loud, knowing that our voice will activate the process of making the plan manifest in 3-D Earth reality (magneto-electric). Also learn to speak scriptures out loud that apply to your situation. Faith plays a huge role in this because the quantum grid responds to faith. We should never react out of frustration or vengeance. Always out of love with that person s best interest in mind. Remember, we are imparting things of higher design.

Eventually, your overall skills will develop to the point where you can ask God to show you how your day will go and show you the interactions you may have. Knowing what may happen in advance can be a tremendous help in being ready to respond with purposeful grace and love. How helpful would it be to see a spiritual attack coming and nip it in the bud?

Confidence is a big issue here. By now, you are confident in who you are and who God is. You have been building your intuitive mind and you have seen how quantum assisted you in your journey for wholeness. You have expanded your thinking. Now, you are ready to plant seeds on a daily basis, knowing greater things are ahead.

'For I know the plans and thoughts that I have for you,'
says the LORD, 'plans for peace and well-being and
not for disaster, to give you a future and a hope.
(Jeremiah 29:11)

Now let me talk about a couple's mountain. A mountain
in the spirit realm is a place of government. Many of us know
that we have a personal mountain yet not so many know that
couples do too. A mountain is an actual place in the
heavenlies where we rule from and release mandates and
decrees from.

A couples' mountain is a place where two people can
govern as a team. If one can put a thousand to flight, then
two can put ten thousand to flight. God is our rock who helps
us sit on our rock.

It is common in many relationships that one partner is
more on board than the other. Should this be the case, we
may use our common mountain to place blueprints for our
spouses in advance of them coming on board. The result is
that they are likely to come up to speed much more quickly
because of what has already been deposited on their behalf.
This also sends a message to the spirit realm that we mean
business in our relationship. Another benefit of a person
seeding their couple's mountain on behalf of their partner is

that the one doing the seeding will gain ever-increasing insights into God's overall plan for their partnership.

So, how does the quantum relationship work for children? We know they have free will so what can we do without violating free will? The answer is that as parents, we have not only a vested interest, but we also have special authority in the spirit realm as parents.

> Indeed, this is what the LORD says, 'Even the captives of the mighty man will be taken away, And the tyrant's spoils of war will be rescued; For I will contend with your opponent, And I will save your children.' (Isaiah 49:25)

First, we start with getting a peek into God's plan for their life. As parents, we are authorized. A part of that plan includes special personality traits and mental acuity as well as their Earth assignment. As parents, we should do all we can to educate them, prepare them, and love them so that they will be likely to accept God's call.

Imagine parents who fully embrace their role of raising up the next generation of Kingdom ambassadors, parents who invest in such a way that they focus on equipping their children in every way. This is in contrast to parents who have turned their children over to i-Pads, video games, and the public school system (without staying on top of what kids are being taught there).

This next generation needs parents who will take their children into Heaven via engagements and build out their intuitive minds so that living in Heaven and on Earth at the same time becomes as easy as breathing. This is the day of the Kingdom. This day requires us all to expand in ways we never thought possible. And we need our kids to find their true selves as designed by their Creator and move forward in a way that honors all our Savior accomplished on the cross.

> *¹ Therefore if you have been raised with Christ [to a new life, sharing in His resurrection from the dead], keep seeking the things that are above, where Christ is, seated at the right hand of God. ² Set your mind and keep focused habitually on the things above [the heavenly things], not on things that are on the earth [which have only temporal value]. ³ For you died [to this world], and your [new, real] life is hidden with Christ in God. ⁴ When Christ, who is our life, appears, then you also will appear with Him in glory. (Colossians 3:1-4)*

> *Train up a child in the way he should go [teaching him to seek God's wisdom and will for his abilities and talents], even when he is old he will not depart from it. (Proverbs 22:6)*

For the children, simply follow the same sequence as we would for a spouse. You may also make deposits into their mountain and show them how to rule from their mountain. The exciting part about all this is that children have much less to unlearn than we do. Also, they have had less time to be programmed into 3-D Earth limitations.

So, what about the workplace? You are there, so you have a certain level of authority. The workplace is a bit different than family. We are aware that God has a plan for nearly every job situation. Use your upgraded skills to find the blueprint for that business. Then speak into it and be aware of any land mines the enemy may have planted to control that work environment. As to your fellow workmates, they could bring any number of issues and spirits into that work environment.

I would suggest that you speak into and over their lives in prayer and declaration. While you may not have the same level of authority over a workmate as family, we do know God's plan is the best possible work environment. We do have the authority to seek God for a plan and then speak that plan over people. The fun part of this is that because you are doing what the Father is showing you to do, you can sit back and watch as God does way more than you might expect.

The final part of this is the geographical area in which we live. We live there, so we have a personal stake in seeing good things happen in a town, a county, a state and even a nation. Never underestimate how God may use you to speak into a locale. Always remember no task is too big for God. Find blueprints for your area and do not hesitate to speak higher design into your area.

In all that I have just laid out to you, remember that we should not be reactive. Rather, we should be proactive.

Chapter 12
Conclusion

As I bring this to a close, I'd like to share a few natural examples of relationships, hoping it will encourage you to be more creative as you invest in others supernaturally.

Some ladies are waiting to be swept off their feet by a knight in shining armor. Others place their focus on status. Still others place their focus on financial security. And some just want to be loved in a special way.

What most ladies do not understand about most men is that what we require to keep us focused and fully motivated are three simple things. Those three things are (1) respect, (2) appreciation, and (3) that we do not have to be the ones always initiating times of intimacy. Men will move the world for their gal if they receive these investments.

When a man hears compliments like "Wow, what a great job!", "I'm so proud of you!". "You treat me so well." That man will go out of his way to change the world for his wife. So, ladies, try this and see what happens. You might just be surprised! To be fair, I already stated I was writing this from a man's perspective.

So, what about the ladies? I do know that females are far more complex than men. This is why men absolutely need to see their lady the way God sees them. We can, however, learn something from Ephesians 5:25.

Jesus said, *"Husbands, love your wife as Christ loved the church"* (Ephesians 5:25). Jesus' love for us is a love that magnetically draws us to walk in the way Father sees us. Husbands should do the same for their wives, which is why we need to have God's vision for our spouses. This suggests we all need next-level grace within ourselves to be able to charge the atmosphere with God's love in a way that brings clarity to any relationship. Male or female, we each have the responsibility to build the other up to the greater image that God has for us. It's a lot of work and requires total Kingdom focus to be successful. In the end, it will be worth it. Father has the plan, so get it and put it into action!

I do know that verbalizing timely words of encouragement, praise, gratitude, and love with heavenly charged frequencies is a skill we all need to develop. Since frequency doesn't lie, we can be confident that if what we release is genuine the results will be powerful.

In the modern era, many people are on a second or third marriage. Few things take the zeal out of a relationship more than being compared to another person. Simply stated—male or female, your spouse is NOT that other person. No one wants to hear Joe or Sue wouldn't have done it that way. Take the time to learn how God sees your spouse and then set your expectations according to that. And do not try to turn your current spouse into your former spouse! Express gratitude based on who God made your spouse to be. Going both ways, verbalizing genuine complements and appreciation can do wonders.

With children the same thing can happen. Children can be turned over to media and entertainment just to make the parent's life easier. Few things crush the image of a child more than being told they are a burden either by words or actions.

Imagine parents who take the time to read to and with their children. Children need parents who pray with them, parents who show genuine interest in their child's day, and parents who just do things with their kids. This is a recipe for success. Normal kids just want their parents and not things in their place if they are trained up in the way they should go. (Proverbs 22:6)

I gave up golf for about thirty years to invest in my four sons and have no regrets. In fact, I probably turned out to be a better golfer once I started to play again because I was now free to focus on my game. I have traveled the world and been in many places. My most cherished memories are the times sledding, playing ball, and just laughing with my boys.

The very core of this book is to understand what Jesus meant when He told us to be servants. It's all about the heart and perspective. We can put the interest of others above our own without being a slave or without being taken advantage of. Let's go a little deeper.

We need to be aware of the effects of the fall. One could say the fall dumbed us down. And on top of that there is a pervasive system in place to keep us that way. My hope is that this book will challenge your view on the Matrix and help you break away from it. One of the greatest potential filters that we must overcome is the cloud that the Matrix surrounds us with. It is a cloud (filter) that skews how we see, know, feel, or hear from heaven. Our light needs to be bright enough to burn off that cloud.

Everything that Jesus did, taught, and demonstrated exposed the Matrix for what it was doing to mankind. He also exposed all those who were teaching others to stay in the Matrix. This is why the Hebrew leadership class was incensed by all He did. Imagine their anger as He spoke about Kingdom being a present reality and then He backed it up with demonstrations that not one of them could do. He also poured salt in the wound of the religious class when He passed on all that He could do to those who believe in Him.

A personal word of caution to traditional Pentecostals and Charismatics who hold the gifts of the Holy Spirit as the gold standard for biblical demonstration without including the atmosphere and culture of Heaven that should accompany those giftings. The giftings and callings of God are without repentance (Romans 11:29). The fullness of Kingdom can only be demonstrated by the level of intimacy one has secured (carries). This explains why the lives of so many who are gifted are often in a mess. Intimacy has no substitute!

For the gifts and the calling of God are irrevocable [for
He does not withdraw what He has given, nor does He

change His mind about those to whom He gives His
grace or to whom He sends His call]. (Romans 11:29)

I also caution believers who attract personal attention from a spirit of victimhood. The power of the Gospel has set us free from this and anyone who will not address ALL potential filters and static simply will not rise to their potential.

The Bible lays out how we should treat each other in the body of Christ; there is to be neither male nor female nor Jew or Gentile, and I am adding black, white, brown or any color (Galatians 3:28). Yet we too often see people favoring each other based on gender, race, and cultural expectations. When I see this, it is easy to deduce that somewhere along the way, that person DID NOT work on self as the first assignment of quantum relationship. When we see this occur, we can't help but wonder how skewed their words and teachings have been because of those filters. The good news is that we don't need to be a part of that group.

Here is [now no distinction in regard to salvation]
neither Jew nor Greek, there is neither slave nor free,
there is neither male nor female; for you [who believe]
are all one in Christ Jesus [no one can claim a spiritual
superiority]. (Galatians 3:28)

So—what have we learned?

- We have been assigned and empowered to change the song of everything around us and govern with a new reality.
- We have been called to bring that song out of darkness by imparting a higher law.
- We have learned that the same system God put in place by His Word, which holds creation together (Hebrews 1:3), is also there to deliver the resources necessary for us to be game changers.
- We are a completely new order of being, created from above, with a new identity, family ties, culture, and resources.
- We learned that frequency doesn't lie and can create very deep changes physically and spiritually.
- Life experiences can create filters that diminish how God's power moves through us.
- We can build our intuitive mind, so it enables a full understanding of what our spirit sees and knows.
- The enemy has a plan to keep us in the Matrix.
- We have a personal energy field that science can now document.
- We can build a new reality that walks in step with Heaven.

- The ultimate relationship is with our Creator.
- We need to fully clean up our mess first, and by doing so, we acquire the skills necessary to help others as we walk in love and compassion.
- We can put all we have learned into action and work with Heaven directly as we interact with the quantum grid.
- God's Kingdom is for now and is not just a religious metaphor; we are assigned to demonstrate it on multiple levels.
- We learned that we can live in Heaven and on Earth at the same time.

So, here's the question: what are you going to do with all this information? You may be on the receiving end of strife at work or in a relationship. Or you could be the one creating chaos and you've had a come to a Jesus realization. Natural or intellectually based approaches lack the depth to effect true Kingdom changes.

My hope is that you will accept the challenge of not being limited to the visible, rather become aware that what we call *supernatural* is just a frequency shift away. Because it is, you have an assignment to be a *game changer*. You and I are called to be on Earth at this very moment of time. This is a time when the veil between the dimensions is becoming thinner and thinner. Let us make our move before the great deception is fully implemented.

Now we know we have access to the incredible resources required to be a positive influence on everything around us. This includes all of our relationships. Let's change the world one relationship at a time!

Be sure to read the Appendix where I have also included a topical list of scriptural categories that you can speak out loud as you impart Kingdom to those around you.

I would love to hear testimonies that result from your application of the principles I laid out in this book. My email is doc.rodich@gmail.com.

Appendix A

[All Scriptures from the Amplified Bible.] Scripture to speak out loud as you exercise your co-creative assignment:

Relationship with Others

² With all humility [forsaking self-righteousness], and gentleness [maintaining self-control], with patience, bearing with one another in [unselfish] love. ³ Make every effort to keep the oneness of the Spirit in the bond of peace [each individual working together to make the whole successful]. (Ephesians 4:2-3)

A friend loves at all times, and a brother is born for adversity. (Proverbs 17:17)

⁹ Two are better than one because they have a more satisfying return for their labor; ¹⁰ for if either of them falls, the one will lift up his companion. But woe to him who is alone when he falls and does not have another to lift him up. ¹¹ Again, if two lie down together, then they keep warm; but how can one be warm alone? ¹² And though one can overpower him who is alone, two can resist him. A cord of three strands is not quickly broken. (Ecclesiastes 4:9-12)

Now the LORD God said, "It is not good (beneficial) for the man to be alone; I will make him a helper [one who balances him—a counterpart who is] suitable and complementary for him.' (Genesis 2:18)

Above all, have fervent and unfailing love for one another, because love covers a multitude of sins [it overlooks unkindness and unselfishly seeks the best for others]. (1 Peter 4:8)

Bearing graciously with one another, and willingly forgiving each other if one has a cause for complaint against another; just as the Lord has forgiven you, so should you forgive. (Colossians 3:13)

³⁴ I am giving you a new commandment, that you love one another. Just as I have loved you, so you too are to love one another. ³⁵ 'By this everyone will know that you are My disciples, if you have love and unselfish concern for one another.' (John 13:34-35)

God's Love for Us

The LORD your God is in your midst, a Warrior who saves. He will rejoice over you with joy; He will be quiet in His love [making no mention of your past sins], He will rejoice over you with shouts of joy. (Zephaniah 3:17)

5 Your lovingkindness and graciousness, O LORD, extend to the skies, Your faithfulness [reaches] to the clouds. 6 Your righteousness is like the mountains of God, Your judgments are like the great deep. O LORD, You preserve man and beast. (Psalms 36:5-6)

But God clearly shows and proves His own love for us, by the fact that while we were still sinners, Christ died for us. (Romans 5:8)

O give thanks to the LORD, for He is good; for His lovingkindness endures forever. (1 Chronicles 16:34)

'They refused to listen and obey, and did not remember Your wondrous acts which You had performed among them; So they stiffened their necks and [in their rebellion] appointed a leader in order to return them to slavery in Egypt. But You are a God of forgiveness, gracious and merciful and compassionate, slow to anger and abounding in lovingkindness; and You did not abandon them. (Nehemiah 9:17)

Going into Heaven

² I know a man in Christ who fourteen years ago—whether in the body I do not know, or out of the body I do not know, [only] God knows—such a man was caught up to the third heaven. ³ And I know that such a man—whether in the body or out of the body I do not know, [only] God knows—⁴ was caught up into Paradise and heard inexpressible words which man is not permitted to speak [words too sacred to tell]. (2 Corinthians 12:2-4)

¹ After this I looked, and behold, a door standing open in heaven! And the first voice which I had heard, like the sound of a [war] trumpet speaking with me, said, "Come up here, and I will show you what must take place after these things." ² At once I was in [special communication with] the Spirit; and behold, a throne stood in heaven, with One seated on the throne. ³ And He who sat there appeared like [the crystalline sparkle of] a jasper stone and [the fiery redness of] a sardius stone, and encircling the throne there was a rainbow that looked like [the color of an] emerald. ⁴ Twenty-four [other] thrones surrounded the throne; and seated on these thrones were twenty-four elders dressed in white clothing, with crowns of gold on their heads. ⁵ From the throne came flashes of lightning and [rumbling] sounds and peals of thunder. Seven lamps *of fire were burning in front of the throne, which are the seven Spirits of God; ⁶ and in front of the throne there was something like a sea or large expanse of glass, like [the clearest] crystal. In the center and around the throne were four living creatures who were full of eyes in front and behind [seeing everything and knowing everything that is around them]. (Revelation 4:1-6)*

Opening Our Spiritual Eyes

¹⁷ Then Elisha prayed and said, "LORD, please, open his eyes that he may see." And the LORD opened the servants eyes and he saw; and behold, the mountain was full of horses and chariots of fire surrounding Elisha. ¹⁸ When the Arameans came down to him, Elisha prayed to the LORD and said, 'Please strike this people (nation) with blindness.' And God struck them with blindness, in accordance with Elisha's request. ¹⁹ Then Elisha said to the Arameans, 'This is not the way, nor is this the city. Follow me and I will lead you to the man whom you are seeking.' And he led them to Samaria. ²⁰ When they had come into Samaria, Elisha said, 'LORD, open the eyes of these men, so that they may see.' And the LORD opened their eyes and they saw. Behold, they were in the midst of Samaria. (2 Kings 6:17-20)

Jesus answered him, 'I assure you and most solemnly say to you, unless a person is born again [reborn from above—spiritually transformed, renewed, sanctified], he cannot [ever] see and experience the kingdom of God.' (John 3:3)

And [I pray] that the eyes of your heart [the very center and core of your being] may be enlightened [flooded with light by the Holy Spirit], so that you will know and cherish the hope [the divine guarantee, the confident expectation] to which He has called you, the riches of His glorious inheritance in the saints (God's people). (Ephesians 1:18)

Open my eyes [to spiritual truth] so that I may behold wonderful things from Your law. (Psalms 119:18)

¹⁵ And I said, 'Who are You, Lord?' And the Lord said, 'I am Jesus whom you are persecuting. ¹⁶ 'Get up and stand on your feet. I have appeared to you for this purpose, to appoint you [to serve] as a minister and as a witness [to testify, with authority,] not only to the things which you have seen, but also to the things in which I will appear to you, ¹⁷ [choosing you for Myself and] rescuing you from the Jewish people and from the Gentiles, to whom I am sending you, ¹⁸ to open their [spiritual] eyes so that they may turn from darkness to light and from the power of Satan to God, that they

may receive forgiveness and release from their sins and an inheritance among those who have been sanctified (set apart, made holy) by faith in Me.' (Acts 26:15-18)

Bilocation:
God in Us and Us in Him

[10] Do you not believe that I am in the Father, and the Father is in Me? The words I say to you I do not say on My own initiative or authority, but the Father, abiding continually in Me, does His works [His attesting miracles and acts of power]. [11] Believe Me that I am in the Father and the Father is in Me; otherwise believe [Me] because of the [very] works themselves [which you have witnessed]. [12] I assure you and most solemnly say to you, anyone who believes in Me [as Savior] will also do the things that I do; and he will do even greater things than these [in extent and outreach], because I am going to the Father. (John 14:10-12)

[6] And He raised us up together with Him [when we believed], and seated us with Him in the heavenly places, [because we are] in Christ Jesus, [7] [and He did this] so that in the ages to come He might [clearly] show the immeasurable and unsurpassed riches of His grace in [His] kindness toward us in Christ Jesus [by providing for our redemption]. (Ephesians 2:6-7)

God's Authority by His Word
Hold All Things Together

15 He is the exact living image [the essential manifestation] of the unseen God [the visible representation of the invisible], the firstborn [the preeminent one, the sovereign, and the originator] of all creation. 16 For by Him all things were created in heaven and on earth, [things] visible and invisible, whether thrones or dominions or rulers or authorities; all things were created and exist through Him [that is, by His activity] and for Him. 17 And He Himself existed and is before all things, and in Him all things hold together. [His is the controlling, cohesive force of the universe.] 18 He is also the head [the life-source and leader] of the body, the church; and He is the beginning, the firstborn from the dead, so that He Himself will occupy the first place [He will stand supreme and be preeminent] in everything. (Colossians 1:15-18)

1 In the beginning God (Elohim) created [by forming from nothing] the heavens and the earth. 2 The earth was formless and void or a waste and emptiness, and darkness was upon the face of the deep [primeval ocean that covered the unformed earth]. The Spirit of God was moving (hovering, brooding) over the face of the waters. ³ And God said, 'Let there be light'; and there was light. (Genesis 1:1-3)

For He spoke, and it was done; He commanded, and it stood fast. (Psalms 33:9)

Translocation: Supernaturally Moving from Place to Place

²⁹ and they got up and drove Him out of the city, and led Him to the crest of the hill on which their city had been built, in order to hurl Him down the cliff. ³⁰ But passing [miraculously] through the crowd, He went on His way. (Luke 4:29-30)

When they came up out of the water, the Spirit of the Lord [suddenly] took Philip [and carried him] away [to a different place]; and the eunuch no longer saw him, but he went on his way rejoicing. (Acts 8:39)

Our Book

Your eyes have seen my unformed substance; And in Your book were all written The days that were appointed for me, then as yet there was not one of them [even taking shape]. (Psalms 139:16)

Before I formed you in the womb I knew you [and approved of you as My chosen instrument], And before

*you were born I consecrated you [to Myself as My own];
I have appointed you as a prophet to the nations.
(Jeremiah 1:5)*

*For I know the plans and thoughts that I have for you,'
says the LORD, 'plans for peace and well-being and
not for disaster, to give you a future and a hope.
(Jeremiah 29:11)*

*A man's mind plans his way [as he journeys through
life], But the LORD directs his steps and establishes
them. (Proverbs 16:9)*

*And we know [with great confidence] that God [who is
deeply concerned about us] causes all things to work
together [as a plan] for good for those who love God, to
those who are called according to His plan and
purpose. (Romans 8:28)*

*But just as it is written [in Scripture], 'THINGS WHICH
THE EYE HAS NOT SEEN AND THE EAR HAS NOT
HEARD, AND WHICH HAVE NOT ENTERED THE
HEART OF MAN, ALL THAT GOD HAS PREPARED
FOR THOSE WHO LOVE HIM [who hold Him in
affectionate reverence, who obey Him, and who
gratefully recognize the benefits that He has
bestowed].' (1 Corinthians 2:9)*

⁴ Just as [in His love] He chose us in Christ [actually selected us for Himself as His own] before the foundation of the world, so that we would be holy [that is, consecrated, set apart for Him, purpose-driven] and blameless in His sight. In love ⁵ He predestined and lovingly planned for us to be adopted to Himself as [His own] children through Jesus Christ, in accordance with the kind intention and good pleasure of His will. (Ephesians 1:4-5)

For we are His workmanship [His own master work, a work of art], created in Christ Jesus [reborn from above—spiritually transformed, renewed, ready to be used] for good works, which God prepared [for us] beforehand [taking paths which He set], so that we would walk in them [living the good life which He prearranged and made ready for us]. (Ephesians 2:10)

God's Plan for Us

I will instruct you and teach you in the way you should go; I will counsel you [who are willing to learn] with My eye upon you. (Psalms 32:8)

'And the LORD will continually guide you, And satisfy your soul in scorched and dry places, And give strength to your bones; And you will be like a watered garden,

And like a spring of water whose waters do not fail.'
(Isaiah 58:11)

'Before I formed you in the womb I knew you [and approved of you as My chosen instrument], And before you were born I consecrated you [to Myself as My own]; I have appointed you as a prophet to the nations.'
(Jeremiah 1:5)

²⁵ 'Therefore I tell you, stop being worried or anxious (perpetually uneasy, distracted) about your life, as to what you will eat or what you will drink; nor about your body, as to what you will wear. Is life not more than food, and the body more than clothing? ²⁶ Look at the birds of the air; they neither sow [seed] nor reap [the harvest] nor gather [the crops] into barns, and yet your heavenly Father keeps feeding them. Are you not worth much more than they? ²⁷ And who of you by worrying can add one hour to [the length of] his life? ²⁸ And why are you worried about clothes? See how the lilies and wildflowers of the field grow; they do not labor nor do they spin [wool to make clothing], ²⁹ yet I say to you that not even Solomon in all his glory and splendor dressed himself like one of these. ³⁰ But if God so clothes the grass of the field, which is alive and green today and tomorrow is [cut and] thrown [as fuel] into the furnace, will He not much more clothe you? You of little faith! ³¹ Therefore do not worry or be anxious

(perpetually uneasy, distracted), saying, "What are we going to eat?" or "What are we going to drink?" or "What are we going to wear?" [32] For the [pagan] Gentiles eagerly seek all these things; [but do not worry,] for your heavenly Father knows that you need them.[33] But first and most importantly seek (aim at, strive after) His kingdom and His righteousness [His way of doing and being right—the attitude and character of God], and all these things will be given to you also. [34] So do not worry about tomorrow; for tomorrow will worry about itself. Each day has enough trouble of its own.' (Matthew 6:25-34)

For we are His workmanship [His own master work, a work of art], created in Christ Jesus [reborn from above—spiritually transformed, renewed, ready to be used] for good works, which God prepared [for us] beforehand [taking paths which He set], so that we would walk in them [living the good life which He prearranged and made ready for us]. (Ephesians 2:10)

God's Plan for Our Children

[3] Behold, children are a heritage and gift from the LORD, The fruit of the womb a reward. [4] Like arrows in the hand of a warrior, So are the children of one's youth. [5] How blessed [happy and fortunate] is the man whose quiver is filled with them; they will not be

ashamed. When they speak with their enemies [in gatherings] at the [city] gate. (Psalms 127:3-5)

Train up a child in the way he should go [teaching him to seek God's wisdom and will for his abilities and talents], Even when he is old he will not depart from it. (Proverbs 22:6)

'For I know the plans and thoughts that I have for you,' says the LORD, 'plans for peace and well-being and not for disaster, to give you a future and a hope.' (Jeremiah 29:11)

And they answered, 'Believe in the Lord Jesus [as your personal Savior and entrust yourself to Him] and you will be saved, you and your household [if they also believe].' (Acts 16:31)

After spending time in the Father's heart and seeking Him about a specific topic be sure to speak these topical scriptures out loud as you place seeds and blessings in the lives of others.

Appendix B

Gemstones

Many have contacted me by email with questions about how all the various medallions that I make could help them. Each medallion has a formula. That formula works with our personal energy field to create a frequency field. The frequency field boosts and enhances our energy field.

The energy set is especially valuable for boosting energy. The medallions that were created by the topic are to be worn while engaging God as it will clarify our own field as we are engaging according to the topic.

Keep in mind that the prices are subject to change, so be sure to check my website for the up-to-date prices.

Gemstones as Frequency Boosters

Since the beginning of humanity, mankind has used gemstones as adornments and a sign of wealth, power, and position. Scripture describes how gemstones serve as building materials in Heaven, but could that be their only purpose? Science has discovered that our cells contain crystalline structures, including the pineal gland with its microscopic crystals. Nicola Tesla once noted that crystals exhibit "living being" properties, with potential uses for sending and receiving frequencies.

Most of humanity gets up every morning without pondering how the universe or creation's fabric is constructed. But just as a light switch is assumed to work, few consider the complexities that make it so. For some, the focus shifts from "Why are we here?" to exploring what surrounds us and how it operates.

Scripture reveals that what is seen and unseen was created by God's spoken Word and empowered by His light. Creation is ordered and kept in order by His Word, and light is its power source, being a part of His essence. He is light, and things are and can be made (of) by light. In that light are countless bits of information, much like that which is carried by fiber optic cables. This tells me that creation may not be

86

static but an ongoing process as His light continually engages the foundational substance of creation that He left in place.

In a perfect environment, His light and those allowed to release His light should have an impact on the ongoing process of creation. However, in the distant past, a cataclysmic rebellion affected this process. That rebellion enabled a dark force to dampen what we see as visible creation.

Scripture speaks of creation "crying out" for the sons of God to be revealed so things can be restored to their original order and balance. This restored order would be very different from the autonomic function around us that we have accepted as normal. In other words, everything is currently on autopilot, which dampens everything around us from expressing things that come directly from the Creator's heart as they were designed to do. We may miss much that was designed for us because we accept this "default mode" of darkness as normal.

In these last days, some are satisfied to have their relationship restored with the Creator as they accept His one and only Son, Jesus Christ, as Lord and Savior. There are, however, others who have been drawn deeper into the story of creation and are pressing in such a way that they have been challenged to use their "light" to answer the call of creation for a more complete restoration. To remove the dampening force so that creation can once again sing its song and reflect the way it was originally designed to be.

Many of us have discovered that a person cannot jump from step one in this process to step ten overnight. There are skill levels to be developed, and understanding needs to be acquired. We first work through the inversion of self to enable a more effective release of that inner light. Then, we can start impacting creation around us.

To be successful in this process, we have many resources to draw from, both spiritually and naturally. Because gemstones both send and receive frequencies and are affected by intent and faith, they are a wonderful aid as we seek to address the fullness of scripture and restore what is around us. Gemstones are frequency boosters that can help clarify things as we seek the face of God in the fulfillment of our earthly assignments.

Gemstones help us work past the static and filters of the soul and body as we seek clarity to grasp what our spirit has known all along. Because God is matter, spirit, and quantum, it is quite possible that the quantum link to His heart was lost in the fall. This would have tremendous ramifications.

I see that gemstones are like bicycle training wheels. They are simply physical tools that can help us clarify what our spirit already knows: the more often we engage Heaven, we will be able to see, know, feel, and hear what is being communicated to us. In this case, *familiarity breeds proficiency.*

Earth has its own operational platform with dampened frequency intensity. Heaven also has its own platform with much higher frequencies and the accompanying intentions of the Father's heart. Upgrading our ability to link powerfully with Father's heart is a game changer.

Let's look at how each medallion category can assist us. And don't forget how faith and intent are the energetic spark to power up what each medallion can do.

Medallions

The Energy Daytime and PM Rest & Contemplation Set $105.00

This basic set is ideal for anyone looking to enhance dream clarity and reduce exposure to electromagnetic frequencies (EMFs). While the full impact of EMFs on our bodies and minds is still being researched, we know they can influence us on multiple levels. The Energy Medallion offers protection by blocking up to sixty-five percent of EMFs and includes carefully chosen gemstones to enhance subtle energies, helping you feel more balanced and focused during the day.

To support relaxation, the PM Medallion helps you unwind in the evening while also providing EMF protection.

Note: Be sure to remove the Energy Medallion by early evening, as its energizing properties may otherwise interfere with your sleep.

The Sleep Medallion   *$105.00*

Designed to block up to 85% of EMFs during sleep, this medallion combines specially chosen gemstones that support rest and promote deeper, more restorative sleep.

The Pain Medallion   *$105.00*

While this medallion was designed to ease those wandering aches and pains, it also does an excellent job of changing EMF patterns that cause migraine headaches.

The Weight Assist Medallion   *$105.00*

By converting personal energy and EMF signals into frequencies that enhance cellular function, this medallion supports weight loss when combined with a balanced diet and regular exercise.

The Focus Medallion $105.00

Different from the PM medallion, this one is designed for increased mental focus. Recently I was experiencing brain fog from a sinus infection and asked the Lord if I could make a medallion to help with mental clarity. The result was outstanding.

Engagement Medallions

Quantum Emotional $155.00

This medallion helps us work on our emotional base and how we process stress and past hurts. With it, we can tie into the Father's emotional realm and reformat our own into His image.

Quantum Heart $155.00

This medallion helps us connect directly with Father's heart. This is important because until we see ourselves as He sees us, we will not be able to function in the full scope of Sonship.

Light/Essence/Arche   *$155.00*

This transformative three-part medallion facilitates a profound connection with both your inner light and the Father's light. It enhances engagement with creative essence, empowering you to interact with the creation around you in meaningful ways. Additionally, it allows you to reconnect with your original design from ages past, reinforcing confidence in the unique, wonderfully made nature of your being.

Engaging Holy Fire   *$155.00*

Scripture reveals that God is Light, Love, and Fire—each expressing essential aspects of His nature. Other descriptions we encounter in Scripture help us understand His qualities more fully. Fire, in particular, acts as a profound cleanser. It has the power to purify us on many levels, removing impurities and strengthening what is good. We all need time in an environment where His refining fire can eliminate the dross within us, leaving only what is true and enduring.

Engaging Glory   *$155.00*

We all benefit from a clear vision of God's honor and magnificence. Like all medallions, they serve to elevate our understanding and inspire us to embrace a higher standard of living. Through these symbols, we hope to receive and embody the qualities of His greatness in our own lives.

The Seer Medallion $155.00

Like its namesake, this medallion will help boost frequencies, so we see better in our way of engaging Heaven. It may even boost a person's dream life.

The Breath of Life Medallion $155.00

This medallion is for the more advanced Kingdom seeker where, rather than depending on Earth's physical oxygen as their source of life, that person relies on the Breath of God. While we are still learning exactly what this looks like, there is no doubt that pressing into higher realms for a higher design will serve us well in the future.

The Ephod $155.00

These are the twelve stones worn by the Jewish High Priest (or gemstones with identical frequencies). This is a true governmental medallion focusing on getting answers on governing self, family, job, finances, and our geographical area. It has a lot of energy, so choose wisely when to use it.

The Mazzaroth   *$205.00*

This remarkably high governmental medallion helps us govern from the cosmos, especially the part where our personal story is written. We are still learning the nuances of this medallion, so feedback is always welcome.

The Morningstar   *$205.00*

Like the Mazzaroth, this medallion denotes an even higher Cosmic calling in some ways. According to 2 Peter 1:19, we have an indication that when the greater release of Christ in us takes place (it's a process), there should be an exponential release of our light and His light in the areas of our focus. This is obviously worth looking into.

Immortality   *$205.00*

We are still learning about this; however, we know that immortality is promised in numerous scriptures, not just Heaven. How do we get there? This medallion will undoubtedly help.

I can say that this is so powerful that unless you have your scriptures ready and your focus in place, it may cause headaches or discomfort. It is obviously not for the faint of heart or to be worn as just jewelry.

Engaging 3-D Reality   *$205.00*

While like the essence part of the Light/Essence/ Arche medallion, this medallion is for engaging the fabric of 3-D reality to see what you have been called as a son or daughter to engage and bring to a higher design. This can be on Earth or the near cosmos as it relates to anything that creation is crying out for as long as it is part of God's design.

The Destiny Medallion   *$255.00*

This medallion is what Heaven says; it is the gemstone that will best help you fulfill your scroll and engage your destiny. It takes a voice print to draw from and then many hours of testing the hundreds of gemstones available to choose from to assemble your special medallion. You could say this is the frequency equivalent to the nutritional workups I do.

Doc's Face & Wrinkle Cream   *$30.00/jar*

This blend of healing and essential oils rejuvenates your skin and helps remove the smaller wrinkles while lessening the bigger ones. Many ladies also use this as a base for their makeup.

The cost is $30 per jar, and unless accompanied by a medallion order, they are shipped in sets of two.

· · · · · · · · · ·

My books, *Moving Toward Sonship* and *Unlocking the Quantum Kingdom* can be purchased from Amazon and Lulu.com

Website: **docrodich.com**

Email: **doc.rodich@gmail.com**

Description

At the heart of life is relationship—first with God, then with ourselves, and finally, with others. Yet many struggle to fully embrace their divine identity and assignment. *Unlocking Quantum Relationships* explores how aligning with God's original design empowers us to clear spiritual blockages, embrace our true nature, and walk in heavenly authority.

By understanding the contrast between the Tree of Life and the competing system of deception, we gain clarity on how to build deeper, more fulfilling connections. Through biblical truth and quantum principles, this book reveals how to move beyond performance-based religion and into a grace-filled relationship with the Father. Step into your true purpose and unlock the power of divine relationships in your life today!

About the Author

Dr. Robert Rodich, author of *Unlocking the Quantum Kingdom* and *Moving Toward Sonship*, is a dedicated scholar of the quantum realm and its profound connections to spiritual growth. With a long-term fascination for how quantum principles can inform and deepen one's understanding of faith, Dr. Rodich's writings invite readers into a journey of exploration that challenges the boundaries of traditional spirituality. This book offers practical insights into how quantum ideas can transform perspectives and lead to personal empowerment and spiritual awakening.

Dr. Rodich shares his life with his wife, Laura, and together, they are blessed with a large family of seven sons and eleven grandchildren. His family has been a continual source of inspiration, encouraging him to explore how science and spirituality intersect to unlock potential within us and our world. Dr. Rodich's work inspires those seeking a deeper connection to the divine through the fascinating lens of the quantum kingdom.

For inquiries, contact him at:

Email: doc.rodich@gmail.com

Website: docrodich.com

Published by:

Scroll
PUBLISHERS

A division of LifeSpring Publishing

www.scrollpublishers.com

Has God spoken to you about writing a book?
Let us help you!

www.ingramcontent.com/pod-product-compliance
Lightning Source LLC
Chambersburg PA
CBHW020914090426
42736CB00008B/624